Failure

ALSO BY PHILIP SCHULTZ

Failure

P O E M S

Philip Schultz

Harcourt, Inc.

Orlando   Austin   New York   San Diego   London

www.HarcourtBooks.com

Selection from "Leaving the Door Open" in *New and Collected Poems,
1970–1985* by David Ignatow, © and reprinted by permission of Wesleyan
University Press. Selection from "Cap Ferrat" in *Area Code 212* by Frederick
Seidel, reprinted by permission of Farrar, Straus and Giroux, 2002.

Library of Congress Cataloging-in-Publication Data
Schultz, Philip.
Failure: poems/Philip Schultz.—1st ed.
p.   cm.
I. Title.
PS3569.C5533F35   2007
811'.54—dc22   2007009165
ISBN 978-0-15-101526-9

Text set in Minion
Designed by Cathy Riggs

Printed in the United States of America
First edition
A C E G I K J H F D B

For my son Augie,
a success story.

One madman laughs at another,
and they each give enjoyment to one another.
If you watch closely, you will see
that the maddest gets the biggest laugh.

ERASMUS

CONTENTS

Failure

It's Sunday Morning in Early November

and there are a lot of leaves already.
I could rake and get a head start.
The boys' summer toys need to be put
in the basement. I could clean it out
or fix the broken storm window.
When Eli gets home from Sunday school,
I could take him fishing. I don't fish
but I could learn to. I could show him
how much fun it is. We don't do as much
as we used to do. And my wife, there's
so much I haven't told her lately,
about how quickly my soul is aging,
how it feels like a basement I keep filling
with everything I'm tired of surviving.
I could take a walk with my wife and try
to explain the ghosts I can't stop speaking to.
Or I could read all those books piling up
about the beginning of the end of understanding...
Meanwhile, it's such a beautiful morning,
the changing colors, the hypnotic light.
I could sit by the window watching the leaves,
which seem to know exactly how to fall
from one moment to the next. Or I could lose
everything and have to begin over again.

Talking to Ourselves

A woman in my doctor's office last week
couldn't stop talking about Niagara Falls,
the difference between dog and deer ticks,
how her oldest boy, killed in Iraq, would lie
with her at night in the summer grass, singing
Puccini. Her eyes looked at me but saw only
the saffron swirls of the quivering heavens.

Yesterday, Mr. Miller, our tidy neighbor,
stopped under our lopsided maple to explain
how his wife of sixty years died last month
of Alzheimer's. I stood there, listening to
his longing reach across the darkness with
each bruised breath of his eloquent singing.

This morning my five-year-old asked himself
why he'd come into the kitchen. I understood
he was thinking out loud, personifying himself,
but the intimacy of his small voice was surprising.

When my father's vending business was failing,
he'd talk to himself while driving, his lips
silently moving, his black eyes deliquescent.
He didn't care that I was there, listening,
what he was saying was too important.

"Too important," I hear myself saying
in the kitchen, putting the dishes away,
and my wife looks up from her reading
and asks, "What's that you said?"

Specimen

I turned sixty in Paris last year.
We stayed at the Lutetia,
where the Gestapo headquartered
during the war, my wife, two boys, and me,
and several old Vietnamese ladies
carrying poodles with diamond collars.

Once my father caught a man
stealing cigarettes out of one
of his vending machines.
He didn't stop choking him
until the pool hall stunk of excrement
and the body dropped to the floor
like a judgment.

When I was last in Paris
I was dirt poor, hiding
from the Vietnam War.
One night, in an old church,
I considered taking my life.
I didn't know how to be so young
and not belong anywhere, stuck
among so many perplexing melodies.

I loved the low white buildings,
the ingratiating colors, the ancient light.
We couldn't afford such luxury.
It was a matter of pride.
My father died bankrupt one week
before his sixtieth birthday.

I didn't expect to have a family;
I didn't expect happiness.

At the Lutetia everyone
dressed themselves like specimens
they'd loved all their lives.
Everyone floated down
red velvet hallways
like scintillating music
you hear only once or twice.

Driving home, my father said,
"Let anyone steal from you
and you're not fit to live."
I sat there, sliced by traffic lights,
not belonging to what he said.
I belonged to a scintillating
and perplexing music
I didn't expect to hear.

The Summer People

Santos, a strong, friendly man,
who built my wife's sculpture studio,
fixed everything I couldn't,
looked angry in town last week.
Then he stopped coming. We wondered
if we paid him enough, if he envied us.
Once he came over late to help me catch a bat
with a newspaper and trash basket.
He liked that I laughed at how scared I got.

We're "year rounds," what the locals call
summer people who live here full time.
Always in a hurry, the summer people honk a lot,
own bigger cars and houses. Once I beat a guy
in a pickup to a parking space, our summer sport.
"Lousy New Yorker!" he cried.

Every day now men from Guatemala, Ecuador,
and Mexico line up at the railroad station.
They know that they're despised,
that no one likes having to share their rewards,
or being made to feel spiteful.

When my uncle Joe showed me the shotgun
he kept near the cash register
to scare the black migrants
who bought his overpriced beer and cold cuts
in his grocery outside of Rochester, N.Y.,
his eyes blazed like emerald suns.
It's impossible to forget his eyes.

At parties the summer people
who moved here after 9/11
talk about all the things they had to give up.
It's beautiful here, they say, but everything
is tentative and strange,
as if the beauty isn't theirs to enjoy.

When I'm tired, my father's accent
scrapes my tongue like a scythe.
He never cut our grass or knew
what grade I was in. He worked days,
nights, and weekends, but failed anyway.
Late at night, when he was too tired to sleep,
he'd stare out the window so powerfully
the world inside and outside
our house would disappear.

In Guatemala, after working all day,
Santos studied to be an architect.
He suffered big dreams, his wife said.
My wife's studio is magnificent.
We'd hear him up there in the dark,
hammering and singing, as if
he were the happiest man alive.

The Magic Kingdom

It's a beautiful January Sunday morning,
the first morning of the new year,
and my old dogs limp behind me up the beach
as my sons scour the ocher sand like archivists
seeking the day's quota of mystery.
To them it's all a magical kingdom,
their minds tiny oceans of good and evil strategies,
the hard traffic of dreams
enclosed by a flourishing expectation.

We came here for the ripening light,
the silence of the enormous sky; to exult
in the shy jewels of sea glass
polished by the tides of the wind,
in the forlorn shrieks and chortling cries of gulls
rising and falling between their world and ours.
To be where it was lush,
lonely and secret enough.

At the edge of things,
in the shimmering spray
and flawless sparkle of seashells,
under the lonely momentum of clouds
lugging their mysterious cargoes all the way
to the horizon and back,
each a wish, a gift
that must be returned.

I never thought I'd have so much to give up;
that the view from this side of my life

would be so precious. Bless
these filaments of sea grass,
this chorus of piping plovers
and bickering wrens, each mile
these arthritic animals tag behind,
sniffing tire ruts, frothy craters of rotting driftwood,
lacy seaweed and scuttling crabs,
after something deliciously foul…

Bless the plenitude of the suffering mind…
its endless parade of disgrace
and spider's web of fear, the hunger
of the soul that expects to be despised
and cast out, the unforgiving ghosts
I visit late at night when only God is awake…

Bless this ice-glazed garden of bleached stones
strewn like tiny pieces of moonlight
in sand puddles,
the wind's grievous sigh,
the singing light,
the salt, the salt!

Most of all bless these boys
shivering in the chill light,
their fragile smallness and strange intransigence,
so curious and shining. Bless
their believing happiness will make them happy;
that the ocean is magical, a kingdom
where we go to be human,
and grateful.

Louse Point

I've wanted to write my way into paradise,
leaving the door open for others... Instead
I am scribbling, beneath its wall, with the door shut.
                                        —David Ignatow

This is where we came to swim
around grassy islands, past dories
and osprey nests hoisted high
under the muted blues, ravenous reds
and lush hospitable yellows
of the wide East Hampton sky—
a place, you said, where one
can almost forgive oneself.

Once you visited late to say
your wife, mistress, and daughter
all hated you, that love wasn't fate
or salvation, but a cold back room
of paradise. Neither of us asked why,
after a lifetime of writing about sorrow,
you lived in a back room of your house.

You loved me like a son, you whispered
on my fortieth birthday, ready
to rush off if I looked displeased.
Our favorite game was guessing
how much truth someone could tolerate.
For P, you wrote on your last book,

the passionate pilgrim through this sickness
called the world. The truth is, I think,
you wanted the world to father you,
to heal the sickness of your soul.

I saw you, weeks before you died,
in the A & P, straining to read
a soup can in the hard fluorescent haze.
I wanted to explain why I avoided you,
chose love, but you shrugged
and turned away when I tried
to introduce my wife. I didn't go
to your funeral, but, late at night, I
bathe in the beautiful ashes of your words.

I think of you today as my wife hovers
like a mother swan and my sons fish
for hermit crabs scurrying sideways
across the surf. You, too, wanted to shed
your life, renew yourself. Still the waves
are jubilant, slightly off-key, the wind
whispers its few small truths to the earth,
and the migrant clouds stretch forlorn wings
all the way to the open door of paradise.

The Idea of California

Yiddish is the language of children wandering
for a thousand years in a nightmare, assimilating
languages to no avail.
                                                    —LEONARD MICHAELS

I liked the music of
his propulsive rage,
his crazy decapitated
metaphors that lived
one inside the other
like savage scroungers.
I liked his wild hunger
to smash the world
hidden inside each spat
out word. Most of all
I liked the rage, and
wrote him a fan letter
after I read his first book.
He invited me to lunch
in Berkeley, where he
taught Byron, of all people.
Why was he, someone
who spoke not one word
of English until he was six,
a nervous child of Yiddish
speaking immigrants, who
grew up in a tenement
on the Lower East Side,
teaching an English fancy pants?

"Dreams do divide our being...
tyranny of pleasure and of pain;
they make us what we were not..."
he sang. We had a lot in
common and therefore
little to say. Asked to read
together in a town south
of San Francisco seventeen
years later, we roared along
the ocean in his bloodred
Alfa Romeo, under foggy
mountains and a glinting sky,
yelling over the wind. "Byron
would've loved the idea
of California, not the place,"
he screamed. He was writing
movies, not fiction, he said.
Why? "Because writing fiction
makes me happy." Didn't he
want to be? "Sometimes it's
more tyranny than I can tolerate."
Was that the idea of California,
to be happy? Around us tiny
explosions of clouds, ebullient
sapphire light, wounded curves,
and the sunken emerald ocean.
"Byron would've thought so,"
he said. We read love stories,
our only subject, we agreed.
Later, in a bar, after margaritas
and all that opulent light, we
wrote a poem, he one line,

I the next. He was seventy
when he died in Rome,
ancient when we first met,
but not today as I sit looking
at his photo in the *Times,*
his black eyes daring me
to write a last line. Our poem,
I remember, was about the pain
and pleasure of being divided
by what we were not, of
wandering endlessly
in the language of children.

Kodak Park Athletic Association, 1954

Nobody wanted the Schwartz boys together
in one room. Arthur pinched while Moshe tore
your shirt off with his teeth. Hymie punched himself
for a nickel, knocked himself out for a dime.
They played first, third, and center. Danny Enright
pulled up on his red Schwinn and slapped your face,
twice. His older brother Liam dragged you by the hair
(which is why we all shaved our heads). Danny was
our second baseman, Liam our shortstop. Tommy
Hildebrand could knock you off the Hixon Street
Playground with a slider (aimed at the cowardly mole
between your eyes) from his roof across the street.
I won't say what his cousin Bim did with his thumbs,
but Tommy was our pitcher, Bim our motivator.
Tyrone Enrique Madison, our catcher, the fastest kid
in the Finger Lakes, didn't wear a mask or pads,
he carried a knife. None of our dads ever came to a game.
We swiped equipment, slid through mud and glass,
cajoled, cussed, and bullied our way through four seasons,
fleeing the darkness inside to the darkness outside,
until the park became a supermarket and all that yelling
a framed photo that said: "Outstanding Members of
the Community." We got Brownie Automatics and learned
a few things: winning hurts less, nothing about yourself
has to be loved; never want anything out loud, or end up
out in left field where everyone is the son of a failure.

Grief

My wife is happier this morning.
Valentine's Day, the kids and I went all out,
candy, cards, heart-shaped cookies.
Gus, our smooth Fox Terrier,
mopes around, tail down, grieving
for our black Lab mix, Benya,
who still sleeps in our boys' room.
Gary, my wife's younger brother,
no longer lives in his photos on her dresser.
He prefers to stand behind our maple,
hands in pockets, trying not to interfere.
My friend Yehuda still drops by without calling.
Right now, he's marching backwards
around my study, making the sound
of every instrument in the Israeli Philharmonic,
hoping to cheer me up. I used to think
the dead preferred their own company.
They don't. They prefer ours.

The Absent

They follow me up the beach,
carefully stepping over tire ruts,
glancing about, stepping into the surf,
sighing, whispering, lagging behind,
not wanting to impose, my lovely dead,
still distracted, surprised by eternal exile.

My Dog

His large black body lies on his bed across the room,
under the French doors, where he used to sleep, watching me.
The vet said to cover him with a blanket, but I can't.

Two hours ago he moaned loudly and let go of his life.
My wife dreamed of his death in Paris but didn't tell me.
I drove home from the airport imagining him at the door,

tail wagging. He introduced me to my wife in a dog run,
stood proudly beside me at our wedding, handsome
in a red bow tie. He faced wherever I was, sat staring out

the window if I was away. If you haven't loved a dog
you'll find it hard to believe he knew it was time to die
but wanted to wait two weeks for me to come home.

I'll spread his ashes at the beach where we walked nearly
every day for twelve years, this gentle creature following me
the mile and a half to the breakers and then back to our car.

The Garden

In memory of Joel Dean

Years before I moved next door,
Joel gave Jack gardening books
and Jack made a garden out of
his passion for geometry, and chance.
He raked, clawed, and watered each
peculiar vision until the daylilies
were good company and the azaleas
were immaculate and dignified.

I used to stand on my side of the red cedars,
listening to Jack's endless scraping,
envying his devotion. I was alone then
but understood love was a gift,
a vast, unbroken conversation.

Yesterday, Jack scraped all morning,
on his hands and knees, weeding,
plucking musical vines. Ask and he'll say
their forty-six years was a garden of exquisite design.

It's best to remember the peonies,
the quaint delirium of lilacs, and Joel
at the back door enjoying the reunion
of cardinals, robins, and pesky blue jays
speaking the language of color and delight,
the language of chance and endless change.

Exquisite with Agony

Only the guilty ask why
they deserved such punishment,
only the stupid expect kindness.
Always it comes to this:
how much pain we can tolerate.
Yesterday, in our town,
a two-year-old girl drowned
in her grandmother's pool.
The woman, who had lived most
of her life on the good side
of this moment, left to get mail,
heard a door open and ran
to find everything once luminous
and unyielding smashed. A child
drowns quickly, silently,
without knowledge of what
is being sacrificed. This is
what we cannot accept,
the idea of blameless loss.
This is why we blame ourselves.
What if it was winter, the pool
door closed, one's need
to retrieve news, fend off debt,
escape the stress of constant
vigilance wasn't so irresistible...
Three generations of womanhood
floated at the bottom of a moment
so crystalline, so immovable,
the mind, once regarded as divine,

the entrance to the soul, tries
to sever itself from the horror
and enterprising plenitude of
its suffering, to free its vanquished
chieftain soul and rise above
and no longer fear its own vengeful
nature, to live a more dignified,
less fearful existence, if only for
a few blessed moments...like
the Efugaos of the Philippines,
who suck the brains of their foes
in order to acquire their audacity,
the mind swallows itself, falls into
a deep black sleep from which all
light is drained, exquisite with agony,
Lord!

Bronze Crowd:
After Magdalena Abakanowicz

"I was asked: 'Is it about the concentration camps in Poland?'
'Is it a ceremony in old Peru?' 'Is it a ritual in Bali?' To all these
questions, I could answer, 'Yes.'"

—MAGDALENA ABAKANOWICZ

Last night I dreamed
Abakanowicz's army
of sexless burlap sculptures
stood in even rows
in a long dark field.
Headless, backless enigmas
with hands, shoulders,
articulated toes, legs apart,
arms at their sides, flesh
hardened to bark,
an unidentical population
of decapitated silhouettes
rigid with unused desire,
the savage bliss of innocence.
An ever building crowd
of souls of the war dead
amid the sanctity of trees,
the mystery of leaves.
A fierce unyielding truth
in their posture, as if
their uprightness
was righteous, a final dignity.

Eyeless, tongueless,
they stood silently waiting
for a word, a gesture...
unable to lift a tiny finger
to protest.

Why

is this man sitting here weeping
in this swanky restaurant
on his 61st birthday, because
his fear grows stronger each year,
because he's still the boy running
all out to first base, believing
getting there means everything,
because of the spiders climbing
the sycamore outside his house
this morning, the elegance of
a civilization free of delusion,
because of the boyish faces
of the five dead soldiers on TV,
the stoic curiosity in their eyes,
their belief in the righteousness
of sacrifice, because innocence
is the darkest place in the universe,
because of the Iraqis on their hands
and knees, looking for a bloody button,
a bitten fingernail, evidence of
their stolen significance, because
of the primitive architecture
of his dreams, the brutal egoism
of his ignorance, because he believes
in deliverance, the purity of sorrow,
the sanctity of truth, because of
the original human faces of his wife
and two boys smiling at him across
this glittering table, because of

their passion for commemoration,
their certainty that goodness continues,
because of the spiders clinging to
the elegance of each moment, because
getting there still means everything?

My Wife

My wife's younger brother took heroin and died
in the bed he slept in as a boy across
the hall from the one she slept in as a girl.

He sold the pot he grew in their basement.
She'd leave work to take him to the clinic
but she understood she had to save herself.

No one saves themselves. Before I met my wife
I'd put on anything clean. My life dragged behind,
like a heavy shadow. I was resigned to anonymity.
I wanted to sleep. She gave my pain a bride.

Two months after he died, we hold hands
across a black sea, trying not to despise
the drunk at the next table, who doesn't
even try not to listen. It's best not to think
about the pain. To shut your eyes and float.

Our kids were jumping on our bed, windmilling,
in love with their capacity for delight.
When she answered the phone she shut her eyes.

He was a sweet young man who looked,
when we took him on his thirtieth birthday
to a restaurant filled with beautiful women,
as if he wanted to live forever.

When we visited his grave, the kids and I
wandered around in a city of the dead

and I could see her down the long avenues,
pulling weeds and staring at the ground.

At night she walks in the dark downstairs.
I know what she wants, to go to him the way
she goes to our boys when they're frightened,
to place herself between him and the pain.

Husband

What could be more picturesque
than us eating lobster on the water,
the sun vanishing over the horizon,
willing, once again, to allow us almost
any satisfaction. William James said
marriage was overlooking, overlooking,
yes, but also overlapping: opinions,
histories, the truth of someone not you
sitting across the table seeing the you
you can't bear to, the face behind
the long fable in the mirror. Freud said
we're cured when we see ourselves
the way a stranger does in moments.
Am I the I she tried to save, still lopsided
with trying to be a little less or more,
escaping who I was a moment ago?
Here, now, us, sipping wine in this
candlelit pause, in the charm of the ever
casting sky, every gesture familiar,
painfully endearing, the I of me, the she
of her, the us only we know, alone together
all these years. Call it what you like,
happiness or failure, the discreet curl
of her bottom lip, the hesitant green
of her eyes, still lovely with surprise.

Uncle Sigmund

hops down the hall and up the stairs
on his one leg and crutches,
boisterous blue eyes
and wild gray beard, a character
out of Chekhov, or better yet, Gogol—
"The streets are crazy with Russians!"
he laughs, "quick, get me a scotch!"
collapsing into our armchair. Gifts
for the boys, kisses for his niece,
my wife, more stories of
freezing boxcars rattling
from Poland to Uzbekistan,
his feverish first taste of chocolate
in a Russian work camp—Cossacks,
Nazis, Polish guerillas, everyone
looking for Jews in the quivering
entrails of train compartments,
in the sodden weight
of the circumcised dead igniting
the fragrance of spring meadows.
The echoing snap
of his father's leg
as he jumped off a train to Siberia.
The smiling carcass of his face
in a moldy pond, his stomach
eating itself one blood-soaked prayer
and cabbage dream at a time.
The currency of sorrow
and fetid black bread,

the ecstasy of his ferocious lullaby
to all the motherless souls
wandering the wilderness
of his fiery dreams, yes,
the eloquent indomitable
momentum of his one-legged
cavalcade of prodigal visions.

The Amount of Us

The amount of us, overflowing,
the enormous overspill of us,
childhood plus the breakers
we walk down to the beach,
always faster, into the future,
bobbing like buoys, minus
the weight of your dead piled
on top of mine, swimming
through the ribbed waves
of my fear of losing you, plus
the heat of your feet curled
next to mine, the angle of your
cheekbones in candlelight, plus
the fragile green of your eyes
in aquarium glass, filled with
sharks eels and delighted penguins,
the squall of sheets, your shining
hair on the pillow, your ecstasy
minus the pillory of childbirth
screams echoing down hallways,
bloody entrails of light bursting
out of you, the downpour of
your fingerprints on the window
blurring the image of us, your hand
nailed to mine, plus the joyous
factories of our boys leapfrogging
the mountain of us, the devotion,
the singing, the burning, the pain,
the beginning minus the end of us.

What I Like and Don't Like

I like to say hello and goodbye.
I like to hug but not shake hands.
I prefer to wave or nod. I enjoy
the company of strangers pushed
together in elevators or subways.
I like talking to cabdrivers
but not receptionists. I like
not knowing what to say.
I like talking to people I know
but care nothing about. I like
inviting anyone anywhere.
I like hearing my opinions
tumble out of my mouth
like toddlers tied together
while crossing the street,
trusting they won't be squashed
by fate. I like greeting-card clichés
but not dressing up or down.
I like being appropriate
but not all the time.
I could continue with more examples
but I'd rather give too few
than too many. The thought
of no one listening anymore—
I like that least of all.

Blunt

I hate the idea of being asked
to bow down before
something in whose name
millions have been sacrificed.
I want nothing to do
with a soul. I hate
its crenulated edges
and bottomless pockets,
its guileless, eyeless stare.
I hate the idea of paradise,
where the souls of Socrates
and Machiavelli are made
to live side by side. If
I have to believe in something,
I believe in despair. In its
antique teeth and sour breath
and long memory. To it
I bequeath the masterpiece
of my conscience, the most
useless government of all.
The truth gets the table scraps
of my dignity. It can do
what it likes with the madman
of my desire and the conjurer
of my impotence. I prefer
to see myself as an anomaly
involuntarily joined to
an already obsolete
and transitory consciousness

that must constantly save
itself from itself,
as a peculiar instinct
for happiness that
sustained me for a brief
but interesting time.

Shellac

My first day in New York City
I found a sweet pad on Jane Street.
It was spring, everyone was hurrying
somewhere tremendous, bursting
with the most eclectic appetites.
In all those buildings all those windows
hosting the most magical schemes...
that's why it was impossible to sleep.
I had to get up, but my feet stuck
to the floor the super shellacked
the day before. Across the courtyard
a beautiful woman stood watching me.
Naked, I tried to peel free
as she continued smiling. It was 4 a.m.,
I was thirty-one, cold, and squeezed
by every kind of vulnerability,
while she owned cheekbones big
as Hermes' wings, emerald eyes
that could vanquish all tyranny,
armies of self-pity—that saw
exactly who I was: someone
who hastened slowly, sought
the voluptuousness of grief,
desired to be far away, teetering
on the edge of calamity. And now,
here he stood, the naked man,
sighing in the dark, deep
in the spring of 1976,

his first night in the big city,
everything just beginning, again,
stuck in a sticky sliver
of fleeting improbability.

The Adventures of 78 Charles Street

For thirty-two years Patricia Parmalee's yellow light
has burned all night
in her kitchen down the hall in 2E.
Patricia—I love to say her name—Par-ma-lee!
knows where, across the street,
Hart Crane wrote "The Bridge,"
the attic Saul Bellow holed up in
furiously scribbling "The Adventures of Augie March,"
the rooftop Bing Crosby yodeled off,
dreaming of Broadway, the knotty,
epicene secrets of each born-again town house.
Indeed, we, Patricia and me, reminisce
about tiny Lizzie and Joe Pasquinnucci,
one deaf, the other near-blind,
waddling hand-in-hand down the hall,
up the stairs, in and out of doors,
remembering sweetening Sicilian peaches,
ever-blooming daylilies, a combined one hundred
and seventy years of fuming sentence fragments,
elastic stockings, living and outliving
everyone on the south side of Charles Street.

How Millie Kelterborn, a powerhouse
of contemptuous capillaries inflamed
with memories of rude awakenings,
wrapped herself in black chiffon
when her knocked-up daughter Kate married a Mafia son
and screamed "Nixon, blow me!"
out her fifth-floor window,
then dropped dead face first

into her gin-spiked oatmeal.
How overnight Sharon in 4E
became a bell-ringing Buddhist
explaining cat litter, America, pleurisy, multiple orgasms,
why I couldn't love anyone who loved me.

And Archie McGee in 5W, one silver-cross earring,
a tidal wave of dyed black hair,
jingling motorcycle boots, Jesus boogying
on each enraged oiled bicep, screaming
four flights down at me for asking
the opera singer across the courtyard to pack it in,
"This is N.Y.C., shithead, where fat people sing while fucking!"
Archie, whom Millie attacked with pliers
and Lizzie fell over, drunk on the stairs, angry
if you nodded or didn't, from whom, hearing his boots,
I hid shaking under the stairwell,
until I found him trembling outside my door,
"Scram, Zorro, I'll be peachy in the morning."
In a year three others here were dead of AIDS,
everyone wearing black
but in the West Village everyone did
every day anyway.

Patricia says, the Righteous Brothers and I
moved in Thanksgiving, 1977,
and immediately began looking for
that ever-loving feeling, rejoicing
at being a citizen of the ever-clanging future,
all of us walking up Perry Street,
down West Tenth, around Bleecker,
along the Hudson, with dogs, girlfriends,

and hangovers, stoned and insanely sober,
arm in arm and solo, under the big skyline,
traffic whizzing by, through
indefatigable sunshine, snow and rain,
listening to The Stones, Monk, Springsteen, and Beethoven,
one buoyant foot after the other, nodding hello
good morning happy birthday adieu adios auf wiedersehen!
before anyone went co-op, renovated,
thought about being sick or dying,
when we all had hair and writhed on the floor
because someone didn't love us anymore,
when nobody got up before noon, wore a suit
or joined anything, before there was hygiene,
confetti, a salary, cholesterol,
or a list of names to invite to a funeral...

Yes, the adventures of a street in a city of everlasting hubris,
and Patricia's yellow light
when I can't sleep and come to the kitchen
to watch its puny precious speck stretch
so quietly so full of reverence
into the enormous darkness,
and I, overcome with love for everything so quickly fading,
my head stuck out the window
breathing the intoxicating melody
of our shouldered and cemented-in little island,
here, now, in the tenement of this moment,
dear Patricia's light,
night after night,
burning with all the others,
on 78 Charles Street.

Isaac Babel Visits My Dreams

The sons of failed fathers have much
to test themselves for...

—Lionel Trilling

"Stalin killed me," Isaac explains,
angrily pacing my study, stinking
of vodka and chicken fat, "not
because I was an admired, if
unproductive, Jewish writer,
but because I made sentences
as resolute as a woman's ankle,
which he (who didn't know
a knuckle from a semicolon),
stayed up nights, dissecting
like grasshoppers." "Why," I ask,
"hopelessly entangle yourself in
the arms of opposed civilizations,
ride with the enemy of your people,
you, a myopic bookworm too nervous
to carry a loaded revolver?" He slaps
his high forehead and groans, "Why
not ask what it's like being a verb
lonely for an object, a self-obsessed
doubt posing as a question teetering
on the edge of its own plausibility,
a rudderless internal monologue
with the sexual appetite of a Cossack?
Why not ask me why I'm a Jew?"

He sits slurping black tea, going on
about ankles and finely woven breasts,
his gray tunic stained with, I imagine,
bullet wounds from his execution.
Finally, I ask something I've always
wanted to: "You saw your father on
his knees begging a Cossack captain
to spare his shop during a pogrom –
can such failure be forgiven?" He sighs,
"In a pogrom everyone's a failure.
Our enemies are where our truth is hidden."
"Well, what is it then?" "What we hate
sours our breath for eternity," he winks. Is
this why his stinks of irony pickled with
savage wisdom? "We're all failed sentences,"
he says, his silhouette bathed in moonlight,
"one big lopsided family of relative clauses
who agree on nothing, whose only subject is
how we came to be us, despite our passion for
knowledge, especially while we were still alive."

Dance Performance

My six- and nine-year-old sons
are performing their homespun
homeboy rap-star angst,
one-handed cartwheels, hips
accentuating the fugue
of hip-hop melody, fingers
and eyes snapping, indeed,
something's astir, appetite
or rage against the great republic
of fatherhood, genetic status quo
pummeled by another level
of fierce unconscious undertow.
Disgruntled darlings banging
pelvises, hyphenating street rant
to immigrant dead ends
where no one deserves mercy
or yields. Okay, I get
the evil eye no one else does,
unprovoked declaration
of holy war: you're okay pops
but stay out of our way!
Inheritor of my father's
ebullient nightmares, I also
wanted the father not
the son sacrificed, feared
our house wasn't big enough
for two of us, understood
in this ancient tug-of-war
the son must kill in himself
what he most loves. But

these kids will need help
emptying the future of me.
When it's time I'll step aside,
twice, once for them,
once for me. Now the thing
to do is bless the loneliness
of their dance around
our shrinking living room,
and wish them, yes,
the very best of luck.

The Traffic

At first it objected
to our slithering abundance,
which was always
demanding to be praised,
and our fretful certainty.
Now it knows nothing
is its fault, it must go
where we take it,
where we need to go.
Its job is to never
be late or early, pushed
about, or trod upon
by its eagerness to please;
to be unafraid of its
own willowy flow; forever
wandering this way
and that, never expecting
to be right or wrong,
one way or two. It
has learned long ago
to sit back and enjoy
the view, which,
admittedly, isn't quite
as important
as was once believed;
to be grateful for
what often seems
a vast purposelessness,
which, though

at times painful,
at least ends
where it began:
an idea no one
can any longer bear
to understand.

The Truth

You can hide it like a signature
or birthmark but it's always there
in the greasy light of your dreams,
the knots your body makes at night,
the sad innuendos of your eyes,
whispering insidious asides in every
room you cannot remain inside. It's
there in the unquiet ideas that drag and
plead one lonely argument at a time,
and those who own a little are contrite
and fearful of those who own too much,
but owning none takes up your life.
It cannot be replaced with a house or car,
a husband or wife, but can be ignored,
denied, and betrayed, until the last day,
when you pass yourself on the street
and recognize the agreeable life you
were afraid to lead, and turn away.

The One Truth

After dreaming of radiant thrones
for sixty years, praying to a god
he never loved for strength, for mercy,
after cocking his thumbs
in the pockets of his immigrant schemes,
while he parked cars during the day
and drove a taxi all night,
after one baby was born dead
and he carved the living one's name
in windshield snow in the blizzard of 1945,
after scrubbing piss, blood,
and vomit off factory floors
from midnight to dawn,
then filling trays with peanuts,
candy, and cigarettes
in his vending machines all day,
his breath a wheezing suck
and bellowing gasp
in the fist of his chest,
after washing his face, armpits
and balls in cold back rooms,
hurrying between his hunger
for glory and his fear
of leaving nothing but debt,
after having a stroke and
falling down factory stairs,
his son screaming at him
to stop working and rest,
after being knocked down
by a blow he expected all his life,

his son begging forgiveness,
his wife crying his name,
after looking up at them
straight from hell, his soul
withering in his arms—
is this what failure is,
to end where he began,
no one but a deaf dumb God
to welcome him back,
his fists pounding at the gate—
is this the one truth,
to lie in a black pit
at the bottom of himself,
without enough breath
to say goodbye
or ask forgiveness?

Failure

To pay for my father's funeral
I borrowed money from people
he already owed money to.
One called him a nobody.
No, I said, he was a failure.
You can't remember
a nobody's name, that's why
they're called nobodies.
Failures are unforgettable.
The rabbi who read a stock eulogy
about a man who didn't belong to
or believe in anything
was both a failure and a nobody.
He failed to imagine the son
and wife of the dead man
being shamed by each word.
To understand that not
believing in or belonging to
anything demanded a kind
of faith and buoyancy.
An uncle, counting on his fingers
my father's business failures—
a parking lot that raised geese,
a motel that raffled honeymoons,
a bowling alley with roving mariachis—
failed to love and honor his brother,
who showed him how to whistle
under covers, steal apples
with his right or left hand. Indeed,
my father was comical.

His watches pinched, he tripped
on his pant cuffs and snored
loudly in movies, where
his weariness overcame him
finally. He didn't believe in:
savings insurance newspapers
vegetables good or evil human
frailty history or God.
Our family avoided us,
fearing boils. I left town
but failed to get away.

The Wandering Wingless

It is of course true that much human activity is the
result of conditions which are unknown to the
participants...

—PRISCILLA ROBERTSON

To become aware of the possibility of the search is to be
onto something. Not to be onto something is to be in
despair.

—WALKER PERCY

God made human beings so dogs would have
companions.

—FREDERICK SEIDEL

ONE

1

I carry keys, multicolored,
versatile, and revelatory,
to my clients' apartments,
where I wander around
their enormous rooms,
sit at their elongated tables,
read in their book-lined studies
under the peachy glow

of their scalloped sconces,
rock before their prosperous windows,
my hands tap-tapping at my back,
my mind, always in between
and on its way somewhere
more interesting, enjoying
the human medley,
the whispering echoes
and colorful plumage
of my fellow explorers
so eager to tempt fortune,

until it's time to walk
Adolph and Napoleon,
who never have
an unkind word
to say about anyone...

2

Here
in the Village
everyone owns
a philosophy of fateful,
exquisite reluctance;
an air of ever skulking fatigue
and deliciously
illicit world-weariness.
On the Upper East Side
they herd packs
of eight up Madison Avenue,

all entangled
and belittled,
with $100 haircuts,
stinking of intrigue
and lilacs. Three dogs
is as much fight or flight instinct
as I can manage.
Walk dogs for a living
and you become intangible,
eclipsed
by a greater force.

I like being the guy
who walks Moses,
Dylan, and Herakles,
at the center
of no one's interest.

3

The morning of my eighth birthday
I awoke to see
tied to our front gate
my first teacher, a Collie mix,
blue-amethyst eyes,
powdery caramel mane,
all golden and delirious,
and Dad, beside her,
beaming. She,
Rusty, was so superior

all the other dogs
ran alongside her,
enlarged,
floating.

4

Dad sold gaskets
without which sewing machines
stopped stitching
the more refined crotches
of the Finger Lakes region
in upstate New York.
He liked to say
he tried to sell God
a second Sunday
but no one buys anything
on Sunday. When
his heart was failing
he'd sit on his bed
staring at his hands, unable
to understand why
they were so angry.
Inside the sparkling graves
of his shoes
he'd stand wavering,
arms hanging,
chest heaving,
each sigh intricately
intertwined

in the infinitely
variegated blasts
of his broken breaths,
waiting
for his strength
to return.

5

The Washington Square Park dog run
is built on an old Indian burial ground
right smack in the middle
of a carnival of joggers, yapping
babysitters, inline skaters
(skating mostly backwards!)
pharmaceutical reps whispering *smoke smoke,*
a swooping armada of endlessly shitting pigeons,
the *whoosh whoosh* of taxis
circling the stoic town houses,
and every time the wind
comes whistling through,
a torrent of fat squirrels
scamper out of
the knurled snout
of the haunted ancient oak
under which
I prefer to stand,
deep in its moist
luxuriant decay, attempting
to pluck slivers
of tranquillity

out of the shade
of my seared brain,

cloaked
as it is
in a desperate hum
of fear.

6

Exactly one year ago,
last September 11,
a brilliant burst
of electroshock waves
zinged through
the surprised ether
of my brain's pink elasticity.
I awoke floating
in Saint Vincent's psych ward,
on a rocky seabed,
an inert acorn, under
a sheet tent, someone
at the far end of time
singing the aria
from *Madame Butterfly*
the way it was meant to be sung.

Is this what it
feels like to be dead,
I wondered,
a false hallelujah,

to swirl, flicker,
and overflow,
never again contrive
to be anything
more or less than
a beginning,
middle, or end?

Then, almost
immediately afterward,
I was put out
on the street.
We need the beds,
the doctors said.
There's a great emergency.

7

There's a new mourner
at the run this morning.
A guy with a red bow tie
and a diamond stud
in each tiny conch ear.
There, off
by the south gate,
clutching the fence,
matching dogs
with their owners,
and sighing. It's
the looks dogs give

their owners
he's studying.
The peripheral glance
of pure attachment
and faithfulness.

Ever since last September,
someone like him
comes every day,
as if to be fascinated
by the routines
of our ordinariness,
to remember a lost,
invisible world.
Soon he'll leave,
utterly slumped,
wanting to wake
and return
to our side of the fence.

8

The thing about dogs
is they don't believe
they're geniuses (especially
the ones who are). They
don't withhold judgment,
cultivate opinions,
mobilize their defects,
become paralyzed

with nostalgia,
or disappear
inside their delirium.
They offer us,
their fellow strangers,
the possibility of
being everywhere
and nowhere at once,
amid the low
and high antics
of our curious proceedings. So
they can stand off
to the side,
waiting, always waiting
for a sign...
from us...
only
from us...

and thus
be replenished.

9

When Dad's heart
was failing
he stopped slamming doors
and shouting every thought.
He stopped slapping backs,
joking all the time,
and pissing into coffee cups

because he was running late.
He stopped crying
in the toilet
when he thought everyone
was asleep.

10

A moment ago there
was a row over plans
for the 9/11 memorial.
Mrs. R., who kisses
her Poodle, Fracas,
on the mouth and says
hideous things about her
behind her back, wants
a garden where one can
disguise reality. Mr. K.,
who dresses all in black
and despises Poodles for
being self-congratulatory,
wants a guillotine beside
an effigy of the president
dressed as an executioner,
while Mrs. B., whose basso
cantante voice is the one
on the famous milk commercial,
prefers nothing. "Nothing is
the most respectful tribute
to horror and rage," she says.

11

This morning
I'm walking a crisp
blue Bedlington Terrier
named Tallulah,
and all the dogs at the run
are making a fuss over her.
The moment she arrived
everyone disappeared.
That's the thing about celebrities,
no one knows how to exist
around them. Everyone
is eclipsed. She's giving off
such a powerful shimmer
everyone has opened up
to her superior force
and feels holy. Dogs
recognize perfection.
They know she's beautiful.
Even in the Village,
where the extraordinary
is expected, her beauty
is rare—what with
her venerable coat,
enigmatic eyes,
and aquiline lips curling
into a perfect ellipse…
if she should lift up
on her hind legs and howl
we'd all kneel before her.
Yes, on this lovely spring morning

let's praise her beauty,
let's adore a beautiful dog.

12

If Dad didn't stop working
and go to a hospital
immediately
he was going to die,
his doctor said. It
was up to me, kiddo,
he wouldn't listen
to anyone else. Did I
understand? Yes,
I said, I understood.
I understood Dad
was sick of working
fourteen hours a day,
of selling himself
one lie at a time,
of not understanding
why, once again,
he was losing everything.
I understood
that he wanted to die.

13

After my brain
was electrocuted,

I couldn't remember
where I lived—
under
the shadow of a bridge
that sang me to sleep,
deep
in the unforgiving arms
of the wind,
or a hole
in the earth
where my childhood
lay whimpering
in the last vacant hour of the past?

Sometimes
in order
to feel superior
to its failures,
my brain lies to me.

14

Find thyself a teacher,
the Talmud says.

I have. A kingdom
of benign,
furry teachers.

TWO

1

Dogs, by nature,
aren't spiteful. They
don't hold grudges.
We punish, elevate, and bully them,
as if they were us. But even
we aren't us. (Nobody is.)

We're all pack members,
performing our variations
of the howl of loneliness,
pleading
with our brothers and sisters
to come join us
in the song of the tribe.

No one wants to live
in the dark wood,
outside himself,
alone at night.

A good walker knows
to join in
when a dog howls.

2

"I lost my sweet Pug Placebo yesterday,"
my colleague Lima is saying,
while watching her client, Percy,
an argumentative Golden.
Mine is a boastful Whippet
named Balzac. Writers are in
at the moment: I have a Gogol,
a Homer, and two Woolfs.
"Cancer," she says. "The owner
told me not to come over,
like she wasn't my dog, too."

We only enlarge their grief,
I think, share your grief
and before you know it,
you're drifting
head over heels
in impermeable darkness.

We're all afraid
of being swallowed.
"I'm so sorry, Lima," I say.

3

In my old neighborhood
everyone was afraid.
The old houses

were afraid of their attics
and cold back rooms,
the trees were afraid
of the wind. Rusty
wasn't afraid of anything.
She would run
alongside my bike.
I tagged along, anonymous.
When she disappeared
I looked for her
in orchards, along streams
and lakes, before
and after school.
Dad drove me
to the farm
where he'd got her,
but the lady said
she hadn't seen her.
But it was Sunday,
when everyone lies.

4

After Dad died,
we moved back
to Grandma's house
in the city. Mother
returned to her old job
filing invoices, and
I found work replacing

DuPont's roof, along
with twelve black men,
not one of whom
had ever worked with
a white boy before.
During lunch I read about
the revolutions of 1848
because I hadn't yet
graduated from high school
and was fascinated by
Prince Klemens Metternich's views
on secret societies,
class consciousness,
the dreams of Parisian sewer workers,
Italian patriots and Viennese students,
and all the idealistic sons
of the aristocracy, who,
when jailed with workers
for whose sake they'd started
fifty ferocious revolutions,
hurling violence upon cruelty,
could find only the words
to say *good morning,*
good evening,
and *it looks like rain.*

I read about it on the bus
going to work at 4 a.m.,
sitting off by myself
during lunch, trying to breathe
through the black fog
of boiling hot pitch,

and at night
while Mother cried
in her room beyond
the sliding curtain
at the far end
of the cosmos.

5

Not one of the three
black deaf-mutes
who come here every day
owns a dog. They sit
under the fragrant decay
of the big mossy oak
speaking with their eyes
and hands. They love dogs
so much they vibrate,
but, like me, they
can't bear to own one.
Anyone who's ever
owned one knows
what owning love means.

6

Sometimes
the blister
inside my head
is louder

than the one outside.
That's when
my brain misfires
and my courage
hides inside
an anxious cocoon,
oversensitive
to foreign interpretation…
That's when
the lies I say
about myself
in other people's minds
echo furiously—is this
why
they electrocuted my brain—
because
I was always standing
perfectly still,
waiting
to be devastated?

7

It's time for Niagara's nemesis
to come by, and Joey's eyes
are dancing as Niagara,
his coonhound mix,
barks wildly, hurling herself
against the fence,
as her nemesis, an ancient
NYU law professor,

jogs by sneering,
every dog in the run
howling in solidarity.
All because, years ago,
the Professor held his nose
while passing Joey
(who sleeps in the park)
and Niagara took
immovable umbrage.

8

On the roof, Little,
who was big and carried a
100-lb. bag of gravel shingles
on each shoulder, asked
why I gave a shit
about what went on
in eighteen-fucking-forty-fucking-eight.
I wanted, I said,
to understand why
fifty revolutions failed
around the world
all at the same time,
to understand something
about perfect absolute incompatible failure.

Smiling, he said, "Yo
a white boy wit pimples
on yur back, on yur cheeks
an' in yur brain. Yo got pimple

dreams and pimple ideeas.
Also, yo got black pain.
It aint kilt yo yet
but it will. Black pain
an pimple ideeas
kilt yo every time."

9

Federalists, dogs
want strong leadership.
On a slow spring Sunday
they like to be led along
the mumbling Hudson,
to the big harbor where
the grande dame, spiffy
in her mildewed dolorousness,
stands alone at the far tip
of this miscellaneous island,
quietly presiding over
the great twin absences
we all pretend
to no longer notice...

10

Last September,
in the balmy blue sunshine
I stood shivering inside
blue tissue slippers,

gray striped pj's,
staring up at a few
inconsolable leaves
on a ginkgo tree,
trying to appreciate
their fanlike shadows
as people disguised as ghosts
ran toward me out of
the screaming tumult
of my amplified consciousness.

11

Weather permitting,
Joey sleeps in the park
because his room
in a residency hotel
doesn't like dogs.
A Korean vet, he has
a Ph.D. in chemistry
and taught in Chicago
before his mind broke.
Just last week,
I heard him
quote Nietzsche
to Niagara: "Many die late,
a few too early.
Die at the right time!"

Not long ago
I passed by late

and saw them
completely immersed
in the desultory hum
of the wind,
deep
in the shadows
of the moonlit trees...

12

Ask any walker
what he dislikes most
and he'll say the weather.
But it's not true. Weather
is never deceitful.
It's not weaker
or less beautiful
than something else.
Not something
that must be forgiven.
It's not comprised
of glass, concrete, steel
and human flesh. It
never pleads for mercy,
cannot be blown to pieces,
cut flayed and stripped
of its dignity until
it owns nothing
but a naked soul.
It cannot be drained
of every last ounce

of its blood…No,
our appetite for dominance
and property, for validation
and self-enlargement,
for punishment and pain—
is what we dislike most.

13

At the run dogs wear
alligator slippers,
cashmere scarves,
handmade wool fedoras.
Mr. E.'s Newfoundland,
Leonardo, wears
an orange cardigan
on which Madonna's
quizzical smile
is lovingly stitched.
Occasionally,
Niagara wears earmuffs,
big blue fluffy ones
Joey found in
a Fifth Avenue trash bin.
They're urine-stained,
but that's how
she got her name.

Hey—this is America
at the beginning of
the 21st century

where even despair gets
a glossy catalog
and democracy
has finally gone public
and God gets elected
president and lucre
is loved above all else,
where evil, so eager
to be a celebrity,
has moved
into the neighborhood.

My brain doesn't care
what it looks like.
It's the brain
of the son
of a suicide.

14

One night, Dad,
because I wouldn't stop
nagging him
to stop working,
ran into my room
and began smashing
my crystal radio,
the matchstick fort
I made when I was eight,
the sheeted easel

under which was hidden
the portrait of him
I was painting
for his sixtieth birthday.
I stood there,
deep
in the doorway
watching him rip
the still-wet canvas
in half,
and that's when
I lifted him out
of his slippers
and flung him
against the wall,
down which he slid
flat as a shadow
and sat there,
on the floor,
twisted,
gasping,
looking up at me,

his only child.

THREE

1

Here at the run, almost
everyone lies to their dogs:
"You're so full of beans
this morning, Cleo!"
when Cleo is clearly
under the weather,
without a bean to her name.
To each other: "Billy,
you're looking merrier,
Lilly will return soon!"
This, *after* his wife Lilly
was spotted in SoHo
with another man's dog
and he couldn't have
looked more wretched.

We all prefer the
imperturbable wigwag
of illusion. We all act
as if we're upright
and kind. We all like
to hear what we have to say.
We all like a little self-rhapsody.

2

At Dad's funeral
Mom told the truth.
Rusty was sick
when they got her
and they put her down.
Dad wanted to tell me,
but couldn't. The truth
was too invisible,
apologetic, tepid,
barbarically beyond
the partitions
of modesty. The truth
was too truthful. So
they buried her in a field
of sunflowers at the farm
they got her from.
They let me look
for her every day
before and after school
for a year, walk around
calling her. They lied
and kept on lying. Dogs
never do but people lie
to themselves and to you.
Dogs are so much themselves
they become part of you.
That's why you never
forget them. The last thing
I said at Dad's grave

was: I'll try not to stay angry.
I understand but
you're a coward anyway.

3

On this one
particular September
Tuesday morning,
I didn't know where
or why I was walking
through crowds
of people looking up
with their hands
over their eyes
and mouths...why
my brain was stuffed
with the sodden seaweed
of grief, singing:
O God
full of mercy
who dwells on high
grant proper rest
on the wings of
the Divine Presence—
in the lofty level of the holy
and the pure ones,
who shine like the glow
of the firmament
for the soul who went
on to their world...

4

Each late morning
Little and I
drove the big truck
to the dump
and shoveled off
the torn-up debris.
Then, sweating, we
stood looking at
the steaming mountains
of trash, trying not
to breathe. A glistening
city of scarcity beyond
my understanding,
where God lived,
if he lived anywhere,
and the dead went
to scour for scraps of praise,
evidence of goodness,
rotting bits of absolution,
because after
all their suffering,
there had to be
something under
all the waste,
hadn't there?

Because I was young,
I said, "Like hell."
"No, more like de US-
of-fuckin-A," Little said,

"if you own nuthun
but a black face."

5

At the run this morning
those with mixed breeds
disdain those with pedigrees,
those with athletic skills
shun those who play chess
and like to dream. Those
who regret nothing
are annoyed by those
who pray and need
forgiveness all the time.
Those who accumulate
and complain
despise those of us
who have little to say
and prefer
the company of dogs
who also have
nowhere else to be,
apparently.

6

Last September
a good number

of enraged electrons
bounced around
inside my brain
as I walked down
one smashed avenue
after another, soot
glistening on my hands
and shoes, wondering
if I was the kind
who seeks God
during an emergency
and then is ashamed
all his life … when

a rat looked up
contemptuously
as if to mock
human misery,
as a man holding
a burning briefcase,
like a souvenir of
my hallucination
ran past screaming.

7

Pheromones,
the Dead Sea Scrolls
of a dog's personality,
are present in a dog's feces.

The hugger-mugger
of over 15,000 tiny scraps
of scrolled DNA cave secrets.

My teacher today,
a sweet Border Collie mix
named Penelope, quotes
from the Qumran texts,
"Our family was larger than we knew."

In other words:
butt sniffing
is just another way
to shake hands
with history.

8

One Friday,
as I was dressing
in the lunch shack,
two men grabbed
my arms and feet,
held me spread
belly-down over
a table as Junior,
the meanest stud
on the roof gang,
raised a broom handle
blackened with pitch,
and said, "It's time

to lose yur virginity,
white boy!"

Bobby,
the white foreman,
stood smoking
in the doorway,
as I smashed
clawed and kicked
my way into sunlight,
where Little sat smiling
on his wheelbarrow.
"Dey was jus jivin'
wit ya, man!"

9

Every night
on my couch-bed
before dropping off,
I read about the frenzy
of the Committee
on Public Instruction,
how political prisoners of
the Second Republic
were secretly tortured
for information on Baden
revolutionaries, about
Count Joseph Radetzky,
and Pope Pius IX (who
enjoyed blessing troops),

and Adolphe Blanqui's servant
who said before the outbreak,
"Next Sunday we shall be eating
chicken wings and wearing silk…"

how the violence of wealth
and entitlement
was hurled
upon disappointment
and deprivation,
upon lack of magnanimity
and the futility
of ignorance and poverty…
until
the world exploded
into a burning pit of rage…

because none of it stank
as bad as boiling pitch at 4 a.m.,
and it was all
someone else's agony…

10

A pail of hot pitch
banged off the wall
on its way up
the pulley so
molten pellets
rained down

out of the balmy azure sky,
singeing my head
and shoulders. Junior
stood on the ledge,
smiling down at me.
I owned nothing
but my whiteness—
was that why they hated me?
Because their failure
was more perfect than mine?
Because in America
color was wealth
and what little I owned
could be envied?
Plucking out each
pellet with tweezers,
the nurse said, "Go on,
scream." So I did,
each fucking time.
Two didn't come out.
"Well, we'll have to leave
them in," she smiled.
That's when
the wave of her
voluptuous warmth
infringed upon
my suffering. When
it was time to go
I just sat there,
on the stretcher,
a poor white dog in heat.

11

One year ago
last September,
in the psych ward
of Saint Vincent's,
before they goosed
me with a lightning
jolt of reality, I enjoyed
many excellent lunches:
chicken with red cabbage,
marvelous vanilla ice cream,
a damn good leg of something—
Yes, asked baby-faced Dr. O,
why didn't I have a family,
a job or pension plan, belong
to anything, why did I claim
I believed only in Dogism,
was spoiled goods, a scrap
of volatile fragility? Why
not ask me, I wondered, why
there was no Constitution
that included the excluded,
appeased the disappointed,
buoyed up the downcast—
what accounted for the liquid
solidarity of the classes,
the flight of the bourgeoisie
from their illusions, why did
the workers turn on those
who died to help them, did

so many diverse societies hurl
themselves into an abyss,
could so much hope, desire
and confidence fail
once again to flourish?

In other words: why
did Dad own, believe in,
admit to, understand
and love nothing…why
was he so afraid
of the benevolence
deep inside him?

12

Because of the
bleeding pellets
I couldn't sleep
and sat on the couch
I used as a bed,
watching Johnny Carson.
Mom, who never slept,
came to join me.
Her fingers were swollen
red with paper cuts,
her eyes black shallows.
Johnny was getting laughs
for not looking
at the improbable breasts

of a blond actress.
Everyone in the world
was laughing,
except us. We just
sat there, silently,
in black and white,
not laughing.

13

The Buddhists call
the fulfillment
achieved through
perfect absence
the seat of truth.

Joey, an ex-Buddhist,
sees himself, he said
today, not as a man
but as a style of his time,
a hymn to the Zeitgeist,
a wellspring of
amiable diversions.

This must be why
he so often carries
an unstrained aura
like a broken umbrella.

14

In the hospital
last September
Dr. O. asked if I knew
what my mind
had against itself.
Did it practice alchemy,
voodoo, try to escape
its personal history
on waxen wings?
Nodding, I remained
tucked away under
a winding sheet
recalling a rainy
Friday morning
when Dad's face turned blue,
his body shivering
on his pissed-in bed,
the light in his big black eyes
flaking as I looked
inside his mouth
to see if he was choking
on his dentures,
not understanding
his life was escaping.

Get away from me!
he said.

15

Sometimes I sit
in the triumph
of someone else's
living room, ensconced
among my extended family
of infamous oddballs: Proust
Nietzsche Van Gogh Byron
Flaubert Blake and cranky
old Kierkegaard who says
such irascible things as: *About
despair it must be said: only he
can despair who is desperate...*

16

One afternoon
I got home early
from work and found
Grandma on the couch,
eyes open, hands in her lap.
Listening to the faint rasp
of her breath, I lifted her
and started walking
toward the hospital
over two miles away.
The heat made her slippery,
and not to look at her eyes
I counted the things she

no longer did: dial, speak,
remember or button anything,
chop or sew or sing
about evil elves and dark
Polish woods, make eighteen
soups out of chickens,
turnips, and a dark obstinacy
she smuggled out of
three countries for an idea
she never understood
and remained too poor
and ignorant to obtain,
for rights and laws
she gave to six children
so one would make
one who wouldn't fail,
who would carry each hour
of her eighty-six years of toil
all the way to a place
where a nurse wanted
to get this dying old woman
onto a gurney, which
I wasn't letting her do
because I wouldn't let go...

FOUR

1

Something extraordinary
was happening
in San Francisco,
so in 1965,
after Dad died,
I hitchhiked
across the country,
my head stuck out
the windows
of various clattering vehicles,
drinking in
the glory of
every last dollop
of America,
all the way
to the far side
of anything theoretical.

Once there
I got so sick
of my voracious appetite
for calamity,
first I cut
my left wrist
and then
my right one
with a funky Gillette,
and swallowed

15 meprobamates
to stop the echoing
in my waxy ears.

2

I named Rusty
after a movie
about a black boy
who had a dog
the white police took away.
The boy watched
them drive down
a dirt road, not
understanding why
he was being punished.
For loving a dog?
For loving a place
his father said
would never love him?
For failing to be
enough of something?
I understood his eyes,
the way they shut
so hard and tight,
didn't reflect anything.
I understood what it
felt like to be so far
down yourself
you couldn't breathe;
to hate the food you ate;

hear your name being
chewed and spat out
someone else's mouth;
want everyone dead;
to blow to pieces
the whole fucking world.

3

In the psych ward
of San Francisco
General Hospital, Cosmo,
a self-proclaimed
psychosexual, who
endured numerous miracles
trying to kill himself,
said from the next bed,
"This scar—know how I got it?"

I, under a sheet,
my wrists aching,
diverted myself with: Heine,
who said an army of rats
would be let loose
when Louis Philippe died,
and Garibaldi, hiding
in South America, returning
to liberate Italy, and Metternich,
counting the hours until
the Parisians ousted their king
and the patriots of Italy

and Hungary were unleashed—
how all the privileged sons
wanted the kind of revolution
and hungry vision
America had (whether or not
their countries
or anyone else wanted
what they did), so that
in the end, everyone,
to quote Cosmo,
got fucked but good...

"I stuck a shotgun
under my chin!"
he howled, "but
it bounced... *live
and learn*, I guess..."

4

Lima, who owns five dogs,
two cats, a blind turtle,
and a deluded parakeet,
knows I live in a tiny room
over the foulest-smelling
restaurant in Chinatown
but that doesn't stop her.
"Joey's dying, you know
that, right?" Arms akimbo,
she's not looking at me,
a bad sign. "What'll happen

to Niagara?" she cries.
"Why won't you own anything?"

Because,
frankly,
I'm not prepared
to do so.

5

Last September
in the hospital,
as my fellow
ruminants slept
in the shadows,
their jaws furiously
chewing the cud
of their dreams,
I wondered: If nothing
is where I come from,
return to, and
am entitled to,
what was I
so afraid
of losing?

6

"Everybody's got
ta show somethin,"

Cosmo said, which is
why he showed
the only thing he owned
to every female opportunity.
"What sort of significance
did yo have to offur?"
I thought of Joseph Maria von Radowitz,
the evil genius of
Prussian politics,
who wanted to be hated
and feared and thus
be considered
a great success. And Dad,
who sold everything
until only his life was left.
"Everyone kills hisself
a little at a time," said Cosmo,
who counted on
his bad luck continuing,
"I go for broke."

7

To please us dogs jump
through fiery hoops,
walk backward, sing,
dance and lip-synch
in movies and TV,
disguise themselves
as humans, run along rivers,
up mountains, across

vast fields of spring,
alongside every kind
of traffic, leap-frog,
roll on their backs,
skid into trees, cock
their eyes and ears...
for us, all for us...

8

"We do such terrible things
to ourselves and one another,"
Joey is telling Niagara
this morning, "each of us
is an emergency readying
itself to occur, a history
of implacable grief,
a World Trade Center
of incommensurate ruin,
an afterglow, a theology,
the fruit of endless labor,
a void, a victim, a revolution,
all joined by accident,
only by accident."

Then, sighing, to me he says,
"Yes, I speak to dogs.
Rusty says, 'Goodbye.
You were a great friend.'"

That afternoon
I walked
only myself
along the Hudson.

9

Last September
every corner
was a compass
that said, Go north, no south,
as I wandered inside
an incandescence
that tasted of glass,
metal, silk, and flesh
rouged and shaven,
and heels echoing
down miles of corridors,
as Dad, cradling
his terrified shadow,
looked up from
the back window
of an overturned taxi
and shouted, "Coming here
was a mistake, everyone's
a failure who dies too young,"
and then began singing
Madame Butterfly
as it was meant to be sung,

as unraveling scrolls
of prayers fell out
of the molten sky,
pieces of oblivion.

10

Today, Roger
is flowing in fuchsia,
which means Ruby
is at the run, instead.
Ruby, tall and elegant,
tells everyone Roger
has AIDS, as if only half
of her were dying. Limerick,
their Miniature Schnauzer,
stays herself no matter
what Roger is wearing.
Ruby is teaching Limerick
to speak French, but I've never
heard Roger say anything,
except when Limerick
got bitten in a dog fight
and the other dog's owner
was screaming at him:
"Yes, yes, I understand,
but really we're all just
doing the best we can…"

11

Last September
Dr. O. asked if I
wouldn't prefer to be
a tad less obsessed
with watching an exodus
of imbecile ants inch
across the voluptuous
wilderness of
my consciousness...
with not being called
quite so often to God's
longest-running spectacle,
The Wandering Wingless?

I don't know how to proceed,
I said, I never knew
because
it hurts so bad.

Yes, it does, he said,
Yes, indeed.

12

It's time for Niagara's nemesis
to jog past and all the dogs
are running as fire trucks
pass, sirens wailing.
Niagara's nemesis is sneering

as he passes, dragging
his ancient righteousness.
Even Gogol, despite his arthritis,
is running. There's nothing
on earth I'd rather do
than watch dogs run,
their tongues hanging,
their ears flapping,
their hearts smashing
against their ribs! And now,
as if to make up for the absence,
they're all singing louder,
their sound so pure
even Limerick's unholy screech
can be heard. And, yes,
I must join this song of the tribe,
this great song of loneliness,
sing at the top of my voice,
my head lifted toward the heavens,
beyond which swirls
the New York night,
each of us, alone and together,
singing ever louder,
until there is nothing left
but the sound of our voices
and the eloquent silence of the stars.

13

Last September
I stood behind

a police barricade,
peering into the rubble
of a smoking abyss,
not remembering
my name or how
I came to be here
in this swallowed place,
where a fine gray dust
swirled
and stung
and howled,
covering all our souls,
which, visible now,
and wingless,
hovered
high above,
finally
desperate enough.

14

In the psych ward
in San Francisco,
as everyone slept,
I went to the window
to see if the moon
was made out of
papier-mâché, like
Cosmo said it was.
Behind me, men turned
inside their dreams,

a pale hand reached
for something in the dark
and vanished. The night
tasted of lilac and spring.
Beyond Golden Gate Park
I could hear ocean waves.
My hands were shaking.
What was I doing here,
in this public pain?
Everything I loved I feared.
Was this what failure was—
endless fear? My face
pressed against cold bars,
every muscle
in the universe relaxed
as piss flowed warm
and free down
both my legs
all the way to hell.

ACKNOWLEDGMENTS

Some of these poems have previously appeared in the following magazines, to whose editors grateful acknowledgment is made: the *American Poetry Review*, the *Georgia Review*, the *Gettysburg Review*, the *Harvard Review*, the *Kenyon Review*, the *New Yorker*, *Ploughshares*, *Salmagundi*, the *Southern Review*, *Slate*, the *Yale Review*.

I drew inspiration and valuable information from Barbara Rose's *Magdalena Abakanowicz* (Harry N. Abrams, Inc.), Bruce Fogle, DVM's *The Dog's Mind* (Howell Book House, Macmillan Publishing Company), *Harper's Illustrated Handbook of Dogs,* by Robert W. Kirk, DVM, and especially Priscilla Robertson's *Revolutions of 1848: A Social History* (Harper Torchbooks, the Academy Library, 1952), a book whose ideas and wisdom helped enormously in the writing of my poem "The Wandering Wingless." I have carried her book with me since 1964, when she was kind enough to give it to me as a gift I can only now acknowledge with warm memory and gratitude.

I want to thank friends who read these poems in various stages: Carl Dennis, Edward Hirsch, James Lasdun, Grace Schulman, Lawrence Besserman, and the late Robert Long, who was there from the beginning; thanks also to Drenka Willen and Sal Robinson of Harcourt, Peter Stitt, Mark Drew, and Kim Dana

Kupperman of the Gettysburg Review, and the John Simon Guggenheim Memorial Foundation, whose generous support and encouragement made all the difference. And especially my wife, Monica Banks, who recognizes the value of failure.

"It's Sunday Morning in Early November" is for Carl Dennis.

"The One Truth" is for André Bernard.

"Talking to Ourselves" is for Edward Hirsch.

"The Magic Kingdom" is in memory of Robert Long.

"The Adventures of 78 Charles Street" is for Patricia Parmalee.

"Failure" is for Robert Pinsky.

"The Wandering Wingless" is for Drenka Willen.

"The Gardener" is for Jack Ceglic.